The Myth of the Walled-up Nun

THE MYTH

OF THE

WALLED-UP NUN

By Rev. HERBERT THURSTON, S.J.

BooksUlster

The text of this new edition of *The Myth of the Walled-up Nun* has been taken from the Catholic Truth Society pamphlet published in London, 1933. *The Immuring of Nuns* has been reproduced from *Historical Papers*, edited by Rev. John Morris and published in London by the Catholic Truth Society, 1892.

Typographical arrangement © Books Ulster

ISBN: 978-1-910375-57-0 (Paperback)

THE MYTH OF THE WALLED-UP NUN

By Rev. HERBERT THURSTON, S.J.

In a pamphlet published by the Catholic Truth Society, in 1892, under the title of *The Immuring of Nuns,* some notice was taken of the oft-repeated calumny that nuns who prove unfaithful to their vows are, or at least used to be, put to death by being built up living into a niche in the wall. The writer of that pamphlet was not so foolish as to suppose that a belief, dear to the heart of every No-Popery Protestant, could be eradicated by any force of reasoning or any evidence of facts. Still he ventures to express a conviction that the fable was sinking gradually lower in the scale of respectability, and that the time was not far distant when it would be repeated by none but controversialists of the most fanatical type. Prejudice, however, dies hard, and that favourable anticipation was not justified by the event. During the course of the following year one of the most popular novelists of the day lent his name to a revival of the legend in a very unpleasant and provocative setting. Seeing that the writer commanded a large public, and that some still account him a serious student of history, his attack may be considered of sufficient importance to claim a pamphlet to itself.

Although the controversy with which we are dealing is now many years old the name of the late Sir H. Rider Haggard will be familiar to most of my readers as that of a writer of fiction who long ago achieved a reputation in a somewhat new province of his art. Opinions may differ considerably as to the literary merit of the work he has produced, but his books, though declining in popularity, are still widely read. Sir H. Rider Haggard was a novelist of great width of range. He has surveyed mankind from China to Peru, at one time unveiling the mysteries of the South African continent, at another depicting contemporary society in England and in the colonies, at another projecting himself into the life of ancient Egypt at the voluptuous court of Queen Cleopatra. For the excursion of which I speak Sir Rider Haggard chose a scene and a period quite out of the ordinary track. He elected to make his readers acquainted with the condition of Mexico, social, political and religious in the latter half of the sixteenth century. His novel, under the title of *Montezuma's Daughter,* ran its course in *The Graphic* in the latter half of 1893, and was subsequently published in book form by Messrs. Longmans.

It will not be necessary to follow Sir Rider Haggard through the various incidents of this unwholesome story. From many points of view it presents abundant matter for criticism, but my present attack is directed against the atrocious invention which forms the subject of its ninth and tenth chapters. The hero of the story, Thomas Wingfield, following for the time being the profession of a physician in Seville, receives one night a mysterious lady visitor. She is wrapped in a dark cloak, which after some hesitation she draws aside, "revealing the robes of a nun."

"Listen," she said, "I must do many a penance for this night's work, and very hardly have I won leave to come hither upon an errand of mercy."

The errand of mercy is to procure "a poison of the deadliest," the purpose of which his visitor thus explains:—

"In our convent there dies to-night a woman young and fair, almost a girl indeed, who has broken the vows she took. She dies to-night with her babe—thus, oh God, thus! by being built alive into the foundations of the house she has disgraced. It is the judgement that has been passed upon her, judgement without forgiveness and without reprieve. I am the abbess of this convent—ask not its name or mine—and I love this sinner as though she were my daughter. I have obtained this much of mercy for her because of my faithful services to the Church and by secret influence, that, when I give her the cup of water before the work is done, I may mix poison with it and touch the lips of the babe with poison, so that their end is swift. I may do this and yet have no sin upon my soul. I have my pardon under seal. Help me, then, to be an innocent murderess, and to save this sinner from her last agonies on earth."

It is hardly worth while to enter further into the preposterous details of this interview. The victim has been condemned to death by those in the Church "whose names are too high to be spoken," but a certain mitigation, *i.e.,* the poison already referred to, has been permitted by them, and it is superintended by "a tall priest whose face I could not see, for he was dressed in the white robe and hood of the Dominicans that left nothing visible except his eyes"! Then there is a highly sensational description of the closing scene, in which there are "mason monks" mixing a heap of steaming lime, a niche "in the thickness of the wall, shaped like a coffin set upon its smaller end," a procession of eight veiled nuns chanting "a Latin hymn for the dying," the erring Sister herself, "wrapped in grave-clothes over which her black hair streamed"—the raven tresses were to be expected, of course, as an artistic necessity, but they must have grown very rapidly since the lady's profession a short time previously—and, finally, in addition to the Dominican mentioned above, a black-robed priest, "with a thin half-frenzied face," bearing a crucifix. All this is very harrowing, and it is quite a relief to know that the prisoner was allowed to sit down.

The dread rites proceed, and Sir Rider Haggard is even kind enough to supply a kind of liturgical formula for the function. "You are doomed," says the Dominican, rehearsing the sentence which had been previously passed upon her, "to be left alone with God and the child of your sin, that He may deal with you as He sees fit."

But the reader will have had enough of this. I will only inflict upon him one more incident, the crude offensiveness of which even Mr. Charles Kingsley would have shrunk from.

> Then the black-robed, keen-eyed priest came to her, and holding the cross before her face, began to mutter I know not what. But she rose from the chair, and thrust the crucifix aside.
>
> "Peace!" she said. "I will not be shriven by such as you. I take my sins to God and not to you—you who do murder in the name of Christ."
>
> The fanatic heard and a fury took him.
>
> "Then go unshriven down to Hell, you —!" and he named her by ill names and struck her in the face with the ivory crucifix.

At the foot of the page upon which all this is found there was originally appended a note in the following terms:—

> Lest such cruelty should seem impossible and unprecedented, the writer may mention that in the museum of the City of Mexico he has seen the desiccated body of a young woman, which was found immured in the walls of a religious building. With it is the body of an infant. Although the exact cause of her execution remains a matter of conjecture, there can be no doubt as to the manner of her death, for, in addition to other evidences, the marks of the rope with which her limbs were

bound in life are still distinctly visible. Such in those days were the mercies of religion!

Shortly after the appearance of this instalment of the story, Mr. James Britten, the Honorary Secretary of the Catholic Truth Society, addressed to the office of *The Graphic* a letter of remonstrance. This letter having been forwarded to Sir Rider Haggard, elicited in due time a reply from that gentleman.

Nothing, he declared, would grieve him more than to give pain to any member of the Roman Catholic faith, but the cruelty of the Inquisition was notorious, and the immuring of nuns in the Middle Ages was a fact which till then he had never heard disputed. Further, Sir Rider Haggard adduced, in addition to the Mexican instance referred to in his footnote, first a house near Waltham Cross, formerly a religious building, where skeletons had been found walled-up; secondly, the Coldingham case, cited in the notes to *Marmion*; and, thirdly, the case of the Abbot of Clairvaux, fined by the Parliament of Paris "for causing the death of a prisoner in an *in pace*."

In answer to this, Mr. Britten again wrote, forwarding a copy of the pamphlet on *The Immuring of Nuns,* by the writer of this paper, as well as a similar essay on *The Spanish Inquisition* by the Rev. Sydney F. Smith. These papers, upon Mr. Britten's renewed instances, were tardily acknowledged, but Sir Rider Haggard, while admitting that such cases of immuring were perhaps rarer than he had supposed, reaffirmed his former allegations, laying stress particularly upon the skeletons he had seen in Mexico, and the verdict of the Parliament of Paris. Subsequently the novel was republished in book form without any modification, just as it stood in *The Graphic.*

Now it is very desirable that the reader should have clearly before his mind the precise question in dispute. Sir Rider Haggard formulated against the Religious Orders of the Catholic Church a definite charge of walling-up alive offenders against their statutes. He did not merely accuse them of treating with cruelty the prisoners in their punishment cells. No one denies that there were such cells for the confinement of refractory monks and nuns. Neither did he content himself with the statement that these prisoners were sometimes immured for life in dungeons, the entrance of which was partially closed with masonry. This would be a comparatively pardonable inference from certain expressions found in monastic statutes and ancient records, though I must protest, as the result of a tolerably thorough examination of the question, that instances of even such a mitigated *walling-up* are, to say the least, extremely rare. But the charge which Sir Rider Haggard made was that Religious Superiors, whether of monks or nuns, were in the habit of inflicting capital punishment upon their subjects by a death of peculiar atrocity, building them up into a coffin-shaped niche, where life must have been extinct from suffocation in the course of a few hours at furthest.

Now it will not be expected that I should repeat here *da capo* the examination of the general question already undertaken in my former pamphlet. To any one who honestly looks into the matter it will be clear that no statutes of any Religious Order have yet been brought forward which prescribe such a punishment, that no contemporary records speak of its infliction, that no attempt is made to give details of person or time, that the few traditions which speak of the discovery of walled-up remains crumble away the moment they are examined, that the growth of the tradition itself can be abundantly accounted for, that the few historians or antiquaries of repute, whether Catholic or Protestant, who have looked into the matter, either avowedly disbelieve the calumny or studiously refrain from repeating it.[1] Let us see how utterly

---

[1] I may note as especially significant the silence of such a writer as Hubert Howe Bancroft. He has written six great volumes upon the *History*

inadequate is the evidence which Sir Rider Haggard adduced for such a preposterous accusation.

And, first of all, we may consider that this writer professed to have seen in the Museum of Mexico—the desiccated remains of a woman and her infant "found immured in the walls of a religious building." When the controversy arose in the *Pall Mall Gazette* regarding Sir Rider Haggard's footnote, I wrote at once to a friend in Mexico, asking for information, but necessarily some weeks elapsed before I could receive an answer. It is one of the miseries of such libels as that which we are discussing, that even though the falsehood be patent, almost infinite trouble must be gone through before the tangle of lies can be successfully unravelled. If some malicious person chooses to show a heap of children's bones to an English traveller, and tells him that these are the bones of infants made away with by the nuns of a convent in some far-off town of South America, what, I may ask, can be done to answer him? You may write to the place in question, if you are fortunate enough to know any one there to whom you can address a letter.

---

of Mexico, as well as four similar volumes largely taken up with its *Antiquities*. He manifests throughout a strongly hostile spirit towards the Church and all things Catholic. Yet he has not a word to countenance the idea that Religious or the Inquisition ever walled-up offenders alive. In vol. iii. page 700, note, he quotes Zamacois for the statement that only nine persons were burnt alive by the Mexican Inquisition during the 249 years of its existence. On the other hand, writers like Dr. Grattan Guinness, *City of the Seven Hills*, page 300, pretend that over *two hundred* victims were built up in the Inquisition building at Puebla alone. This ridiculous story is contradicted in the most formal manner by the archæologist, Señor Agreda, the present Director of the National Museum in Mexico. The remains discovered there and in the convent of Santo Domingo, were simply those of the monks who had been buried in a crypt below and behind the High Altar. See letter in the *Pall Mall Gazette* for January 25th, 1894.

If, again, it should happen that your friend can afford to devote time to the inquiry, if he should chance to be a man who is able and willing to make such an investigation, he may go about, he may inquire here and there, and examine such records as are accessible; and even then, after endless trouble, the sum total of his report will be that he has *not* found any justification for the statement which has been made. For this reason it seemed to me that we were warranted in treating all such appeals to what had been seen or done in a country like Mexico as mere travellers' tales, until the facts alleged could be authenticated in such a way that investigation was rendered possible. If Sir Rider Haggard had given his readers an extract from the official catalogue of the Museum of Mexico in the original Spanish, or if he had named the authority who vouched for the discovery of the remains, he would at least have done something to shift the responsibility of the libel from off his own shoulders; as it was, we had to look to him for proof, and no atom of proof was forthcoming beyond bare assertion.

While waiting for the arrival of definite information from Mexico, a lively correspondence was carried on for some weeks in the *Pall Mall Gazette,* in the course of which Sir Rider Haggard declared his intention of consulting certain antiquarian friends and students of history. As a result of this appeal to authority a letter was addressed by him to the *Pall Mall Gazette* (January 31st, 1894), containing amongst other things the following passage:—

> Before passing to this subject, however, I wish to say that I am now convinced that I was in error when I stated in my letter to Mr. Britten, of August 9th, that I believed the evidence of history to prove that nuns who had broken their vows had been immured in the walls of convents. This opinion I arrived at too hastily, after consulting such authorities as I had at hand; but further research and communications that I have

received from gentlemen learned in ecclesiastical history show me that whether or not the taking of "the life of a nun for a grave moral transgression might be conceivably defended as an act of judicial authority," as Father Thurston suggests in his article,[1] there is no proof that so barbarous a punishment was ever enforced, at any rate in this country.

A few words may be said later on as to the ground over which the discussion travelled before Sir Rider Haggard reached this very desirable conclusion. For the present it will be better to keep to the question of the mummy in the Museum of Mexico, with regard to which no retractation had so far been made, at any rate, in formal terms. It took some little time to communicate with my friends in Mexico, and the correspondence in the *Pall Mall Gazette* was over before their replies were received; but the replies were full and satisfactory when they did come. It would be impossible to print here at length the autograph statements which my friend obtained for me from four of the most distinguished archæologists in Mexico, including Señor Icazbalceta, the then president of the Mexican Academy. Suffice it to say that there was an unanimous expression of opinion denying in the most emphatic terms the existence of any custom of immuring, whether in the case of nuns or of prisoners of the Inquisition. I will, however, translate the reply, which was not only given privately, but printed in *El Tiempo,* the principal daily newspaper of Mexico, on March 6th, 1894. It emanated from a leading official of the Museum with the authority of the Director, and was printed in connection with a formal letter of inquiry, which last, after quoting Sir Rider Haggard's footnote, proceeded as follows:—

---

[1] The article referred to will be found in *The Month*, January, 1894. I must refer the reader to the text of that article to discover the very innocent sense in which this "suggestion" was made.

These assertions of Sir Rider Haggard have given rise to a controversy in the London Press, in the course of which the novelist has made public the following additional details: (1) that the place in which the remains referred to were walled-up was a convent of nuns in this city of Mexico[1] (2) that the marks of the cord, the intrinsic evidence of the fact of the immuring, were visible upon the ankles; and (3) that besides the remains of the young woman referred to, there were to be seen in the Museum of Mexico those of another woman, without a child, who had also been walled-up alive in a convent.[2]

As you understand, Señor Agreda, this question of the walling-up of nuns is one of great interest for the history of Mexico, and if there existed in the museum such conclusive proofs of the fact as are alleged, the matter would be definitely settled. On this account I venture to hope that you will be so kind as to tell me:—

(*a*) Whether there exists for the public any printed catalogue of the objects preserved in the museum.

(*b*) What is known of the origin of these mummies, and in particular whether there appear upon them the marks of the cord spoken of.

---

[1] This statement is clearly made by Sir Rider Haggard in his communication to the *Pall Mall Gazette* of January 17th, as well as in his letter to Mr. Britten, of August 9th. By the 26th of January, however, he had come to the conclusion that the remains were found, not in Mexico, but in Puebla, a fact which shows conclusively that Sir Rider Haggard published his footnote first and found evidence to justify it afterwards. The date of Don Manuel Solé's letter makes it clear that he could not, when he wrote, have seen Sir Rider Haggard's later account of the matter, printed only on January 31st.

[2] With regard to this second body, Sir Rider Haggard speaks more guardedly. He says: "It was *alleged* to have been found in the walls of a convent" (*Pall Mall Gazette,* January 17th).

A reply to these questions will earn the gratitude of your obedient servant, etc.

MANUEL SOLÉ.

Reply to the Rev. Don Manuel Solé.
NATIONAL MUSEUM OF MEXICO,
February 28th, 1894.

HONOURED SIR,—In compliance with your desire to obtain definite information about certain mummies exhibited in one of the halls of this institution, I, as librarian of the same, and with the authorization of the Director *ad interim,* beg to make the following statement.

There exists no printed catalogue of the National Museum which is sold to the public, because that which was made in 1882, extending only to the departments of history and archæology, is completely out of print, and there only remain in the establishment such copies as are included in the second volume of the *Anales;* and in this catalogue the mummies do not appear. Two or more catalogues have been printed for the use of foreigners,[1] but without any co-operation on the part of the officials of the institution and without the sanction of the Director. Consequently, as they have been made by persons who may be wholly incompetent, and who have no knowledge of the antecedents of the objects exhibited, no reliance can be placed upon them.

There are four mummies in the National Museum, and they stand open to public view in the department of anthropology. Two are those of adults and the other two of children. Of the two first, one is the body of a woman. It was taken from one of the tombs of the cemetery (*panteon*)[2] of Our

---

[1] [One of these, printed in English in 1884, I have seen. It contains no mention of the mummies.]

[2] [The word *panteon* is commonly used in Mexico to designate a cem-

Lady of the Angels, and the chaplain of that sacred enclosure (*santuario*) stated that it was the body of the Señora Dona Luz Urbina, a person whom he had known and with whom he had conversed. The hair is still braided in plaits, which makes it clear that the said lady was not a Religious, but a secular person, since Religious did not use plaits, besides the fact that they always wore their hair cut extremely short. There are marks upon the ankles which show that they have been tied together, but this is not anything extraordinary, since in some cases it was the custom to tie the ankles of a corpse, and also the arms. I have myself seen this done many times. Over the head is placed a ticket, with these words: "Human body naturally desiccated. Panteon de los Angeles, Mexico."

The other adult body is that of a man. His name is unknown, and it is believed to have been brought from the same cemetery, or from that of the Campo Florido, or from that of San Diego. On the ticket inside the case (*nicho*) are the words: "Human body naturally desiccated. Mexico."

The two bodies of children have no connection whatever with those of the adults. They were extracted from other tombs in the cemeteries named, and brought to the museum on a different occasion from the adults, and if they were placed in the same cases in which the others are preserved, it was because there was no other place in which they could be conveniently exhibited.

As for the practice of immuring, I beg to state that in this country no such punishment has ever been used either by the Inquisition or by the Religious Orders of men, or by nuns. In the convents of Religious of both sexes there were prisons, but prisons so constructed that the health of the persons confined in them suffered no hurt. They had light more than sufficient

---

etery: *El Panteon de Dolores, El Panteon Frances,* etc.]

to read, to write, and to recite the Divine Office. There was a bed to sleep upon, a table to eat and to write at, etc. On feast days they left their cells to comply with the precept of hearing Mass, and also on the titular festival of the convent, and on other principal feasts of the Order, in order to take part in these solemnities together with the rest of the community.

At the beginning of the year 1861 much excitement was caused in this city by the discovery of some mummies in the Convent of Santo Domingo. It was pretended that these were the victims put to death by the Religious, or by the Inquisition, and a foreigner named Campi purchased some from the Government, and upon this false idea conveyed them out of the country as a commercial speculation. The corpses in question were those of Religious who had died in the convent, as was shown by their habit, their tonsures, etc. The bodies were so well preserved because the tombs in which they had been deposited were very dry, and they were not found in the cloister, but in the charnel-house of the cemetery (*en el osario del panteon*), in which place I had myself seen them many times before. …

JOSÉ MARIA DE AGREDA Y SANCHEZ.

It is unnecessary to print the rest of the letter or the editorial comments which accompanied it. I may add, however, that a series of open letters, signed "Adams," were subsequently published in the same newspaper,[1] charging a certain Protestant minister in Mexico, the representative of some American Bible Society, with fabricating this story repeated in Sir Rider Haggard's footnote. With the truth or falsehood of this personal accusation we are not now concerned, but in reference to these same letters of "Ad-

---

[1] They appeared eventually in book form under the title *Las Armas del Protestantismo,* Mexico, 1894.

ams," it is interesting to quote an expression of opinion from *The Two Republics,* the only English newspaper published in Mexico, and presumably exempt from clerical influences.

A writer who signs himself "Adams" is printing in the *Tiempo* a series of two-column letters addressed to Mr. Rider Haggard, the distinguished English novelist. Just what Mr. "Adams" aims at is not yet apparent, although his eleventh epistle has been given to an anxious public. Now that he has passed the introductory to his subject, it seems that he is approaching a point when he will inform us that he intends to assail that often refuted statement of Mr. Haggard's relative to the mummies in the National Museum. He might have saved himself this trouble, as the Mexican Press has printed the letter from the Librarian of the Museum, in which he shows in a single column that Mr. Haggard had been guyed or else had sat at the feet of an ignoramus. All this the world now knows without being again told by Mr. "Adams." It may be, however, that when Mr. "Adams" finally reaches the pith of the history, it will be found that he is not discussing the mummies at all. Time will tell.[1]

So much for the facts regarding Sir Rider Haggard's "desiccated body of a walled-up nun." And with this conspicuous instance before our eyes I cannot refrain from insisting once more that all similar stories are utterly untrustworthy. There are so many causes which may explain the presence of dried-up human remains in walls and niches. For instance, in almost every part of the globe bodies have been found enclosed in masonry in accordance with a world-wide superstition familiar to students of folklore.[2] The imagination of the people, amongst whom such vague traditions lie dormant, is easily roused to connect them with any unpopular

---

[1]   *The Two Republics,* Mexico, June 3rd, 1894.
[2]   See Liebrecht's *Zur Volkskunde,* pp. 284–296; *Revue Celtique,* vol. iv. p. 120.

or mysterious object, and though Religious incur the largest share of these calumnies, they do not enjoy a monopoly.

> It is not [says a reviewer of Mr. Tylor's *Primitive Culture,* in *Nature,* June 15th, 1871] many years since the present Lord Leigh was accused of having built an obnoxious person—one account, if we remember right, said eight obnoxious persons— into the foundations of a bridge at Stoneleigh. Of course so preposterous a charge carried on its face its own sufficient refutation, but the fact that it was brought at all is a singular instance of the almost incredible vitality of old traditions. The real origin of a story such as this dates from a time when the foundations of bridges, palaces and temples were really laid upon human victims, a practice the tradition of which is handed down to us in the romance of Merlin, and a thousand other legends, to be finally embalmed for the benefit of posterity in Mr. Tylor's volumes.

More recently a writer in the *Academy* speaks in much the same terms.

> It has been a common superstition in almost all parts of Europe that a new building can only be made secure by sprinkling the foundation with a child's blood, or by walling-up a girl alive in the masonry.[1]

But even this is only half the case, for the practice of upright interment has been familiar at many different epochs and in many different places. Whole families, it would seem, in England, have retained this tradition, like the Pagets of Drayton, the Hobarts

---

[1] *Academy*, July 31st, 1886, p. 73, Ed. Peacock, F.S.A., in *Dublin Review*, January, 1889, p. 50.

at Blickling, the Claphams, the Mauleverers,[1] etc. On the other hand, many of the cases are isolated and apparently motiveless. There is one such burial in an upright position at Breckles chancel in Norfolk,[2] where a nearly circular slab is let into the wall with the motto:

Stat ut vixit erecta.

I have spoken elsewhere of the burial customs of the Capuchins, but I cannot resist the temptation of setting down a fuller account of one of these strange crypts, given by a bigoted Protestant at the end of the 18th century:—

> This morning we went to see a celebrated convent of Capuchins, about a mile without the city. It contains nothing very remarkable but the burial place, which is indeed a great curiosity. This is a vast subterraneous apartment, divided into large commodious galleries, the walls on each side of which are hollowed into a variety of niches, as if intended for a great collection of statues; these niches, instead of statues, are all filled with dead bodies set upright upon their legs, and fixed by the back to the inside of the niche; their number is about three hundred. They are all dressed in the clothes they usually wore, and form a most respectable and venerable assembly. The skin and muscles, by a certain preparation, become as dry and hard as a piece of stock-fish, and although many of them have been here upwards of two hundred and fifty years, yet none are reduced to skeletons; the muscles indeed appear in some to be a good deal more shrunk than in others, probably because these persons had been more attenuated at the time of their death.

---

[1] See *Notes and Queries*, 4th Series, vol. v. p. 249.
[2] *Ibid.*, p. 349.

Here the people of Palermo pay daily visits to their deceased friends, and recall with pleasure and regret the scenes of their past life; here they familiarize themselves with their future state, and choose the company they would wish to keep in the other world. It is a common thing to make choice of a niche, and to try if the body fits it, that no alterations may be necessary after they are dead: and sometimes, by way of a voluntary penance, they accustom themselves to stand for hours in these niches.[1]

If this was the case in Southern Europe, much more was it the custom in Mexico, for the dead in religious houses to be interred in the church walls, or in the walls of the convent itself. As Mr. Wilfrid Amor, a civil engineer, eighteen years resident in Mexico, explains in a letter to the *Pall Mall Gazette* for January 27th, inhumation is difficult in that country because water begins to accumulate in any excavation a few feet below the surface. Hence the dead are buried in niches of masonry work, either horizontal or vertical. Señor Agreda attests that he had himself seen the bodies of hundreds of Religious naturally desiccated in the crypt below the Church of Santo Domingo, the very place where certain Protestant missionaries afterwards pretended to have discovered the walled-up nuns.

It seems clear from this that not only Religious, but secular persons were often buried in this way. The same thing is attested by another writer in *Notes and Queries,* who tells us that: "Besides the friars and those who have chosen to be buried in the habit, there are members of other monastic societies and ladies in full dress."[2]

I have spoken above of the discussion to which the novelist's

---

[1] P. Brydone, F.R.S., *Tour through Sicily and Malta.* Two vols. London, 1774. Vol. ii. p. 107.
[2] 4th Series, vol. v. p. 249.

footnote and Mr. Britten's challenge gave rise. One or two episodes in that discussion deserve further comment. When Sir Rider Haggard, after perpetrating the libel complained of, learnt, to his great surprise, from the Secretary of the Catholic Truth Society, that Catholics were unreasonable enough to deny and resent such charges, he naturally began to bethink himself how he might justify the accusations he had made. The *Encyclopædia Britannica* is a very convenient storehouse of information, and in an article on "Monachism," by that eminent canon-lawyer and veracious historian, Dr. R. F. Littledale, Sir Rider Haggard lighted upon some useful references.[1] He found there that in 1763, the Parliament of Paris fined the Abbot of Clairvaux forty thousand crowns for causing the death of a prisoner in an *in pace*. That Sir Rider Haggard derived his information from this source appears first from the coincidence that he, like Dr. Littledale, speaks without italics of the "Parlement of Paris,"; and, secondly, from the fact that in borrowing his information from Dr. Littledale, he has also borrowed one of those characteristic inaccuracies which invariably attend the citations of that author. The fact is, Dr. Littledale, in his article on Monachism, has drawn largely, although without acknowledgment, from the article "Religieux," in the *Dictionnaire Universel* of Larousse. That writer, a bitter enemy of religion, states correctly that the *Abbaye* of Clairvaux was condemned to pay a fine of forty thousand crowns for the Religious for whose death the monastery was held responsible. Dr. Littledale has translated the word *Abbaye* Abbot, even in spite of the feminine participle which follows, and Sir Rider Haggard, suspecting nothing, copied his mistake.

And here I cannot refrain from a word of comment upon the *mala fides* which has recourse to a writer of the type of Larousse

---

[1] This article, which appeared in the 9th Edition of the *Encyclopædia,* is not retained in that issued in 1910.

for information about the discipline of the Catholic Church. In this same article "Religieux," the author, after insinuating the existence of a widespread corruption among the convents of the eighteenth century, goes on to declare that this state of things was by no means new, but had existed amongst Religious from the beginning. Even in the time of St. Basil, he says, we find him inveighing against the license of the monasteries; and St. John Chrysostom would have had nuns who broke their vow of chastity not only put to death, but even cut in two, or buried alive with the partner of their crimes. Most pious Anglicans, I fancy, will be somewhat shocked to find St. John Chrysostom in company with the fanatical abbots and abbesses who wall-up their Religious alive. But French rationalists are so wanting in discrimination they never know where to draw the line.

Of course the great orator's words do not really bear the meaning attributed to them. In the heat of his indignation he undoubtedly says that incontinent Religious *deserve to* be sawn in two, or buried alive, just as a political speaker, or pamphleteer, at the present day, may sometimes say of his opponents that hanging is too good for them. But the Saint makes it clear, a few sentences lower down, that he has no more idea of his suggestion being acted upon than the modern politician has. "We cannot act as Phinees did," he says, referring to Numbers xxv. 11, "it is not permitted to us to seize the knife (οὐ λὰρ ἐφεῖται ἁρπάσαι μάχαιραυ) and transfix such offenders with the spear. We endure the same provocation, but we do not take the same action. We find relief for our anguish in other ways, by our sighs and tears."

But to return to the case of the monks of Clairvaux. Sir Rider Haggard, after being confronted with the Catholic Truth Society's pamphlet, thought it expedient to throw overboard the nun of Coldingham, but he fell back upon the French example. "I dare say," he was good enough to own in his second letter to Mr. Britten, "that cases of immuring were rarer than is supposed, but that they existed, the instance of the fining of the Abbot of Clairvaux, after due investigation by the Parliament of Paris, seems to prove conclusively."

Sir Rider Haggard, as I have said, obtains his information about this judicial investigation of the Parliament of Paris from Dr. Littledale in the *Encyclopædia*. Dr. Littledale has borrowed it from Larousse. Larousse, in turn, has taken his brief account of it verbatim from M. Paul Boiteau, who, in his work, *L'État de France en* 1789, writes thus: "En 1763, l'Abbaye de Clairvaux était condamnée par le Parlement de Paris à 40,000 écus d'amende pour avoir *laissé périr* des religieux dans les culs de basse fosse d'un *in pace*."[1] In other words, the monastery of Clairvaux collectively was fined by the then Parliament of Paris for having allowed some Religious to die, presumably of neglect, or insufficient nourishment, in the dungeons of the monastery prison. It may be pointed out that this in any case is something quite different from the walling-up of a monk in a niche. But let that pass. What is the truth of the story?

Through the kindness of a friend information has come to me on the authority of two of the *Archivistes aux Archives Nationales* in Paris, Messrs. Legrand and Delachenal, that the original documents of the process either no longer exist or cannot be found. However, all that is known of the case is fully summarized in Guyot, *Répertoire Universel de Jurisprudence Civile,* Paris, 1784, vol. xiii. pp. 767–770, and that is abundantly sufficient for our purpose. I have consulted the work referred to and find:—

(1) That the case was decided not by the *Parlement de Paris* but by an arrêt of the *Grand Conseil,* a sort of high court of appeal.

(2) That it was not a criminal prosecution but a civil suit for damages. The monk who died in prison had run away from the

---

[1] P. 194. It is noteworthy that in the 2nd Edition of his work, M. Paul Boiteau has left out all mention of this case.

cloister many years before. He had married in the world, but was arrested as an apostate in 1750, and died in confinement the next year. The action was brought ten years afterwards by his widow, on the plea that her husband had never properly made his profession, was no true apostate, and consequently had been unjustly imprisoned.

(3) That the wife herself had also been imprisoned at the same time, and remained in confinement for three years before she was set at liberty.

(4) That damages were awarded in two equal penalties—one presumably for the unjust imprisonment of the husband, the other for that of the wife.

(5) That no word in Guyot's summary, from beginning to end, suggests that any unusual severity was shown towards the prisoners, or that her husband had died from any but natural causes.

There is very little to be said of Sir Rider Haggard's only other piece of evidence, the "house near Waltham Cross that was once devoted to religious purposes." "Here," as he stated in the first of his letters, "I was shown a dungeon in which, I am informed, the skeletons of two women have been found walled-up, and with them an earthenware pitcher."

It will perhaps be admitted that this testimony is somewhat vague, and though the writer was asked to give references to some contemporary account of the discovery, he was unable to do so. He simply declared that the house, he thought, was known as Cardinal Wolsey's house. "Beneath the building," he continues, "is a very curious crypt built in an ecclesiastical style, that from difficulty of access I judged to have been used for purposes of secret worship in times of persecution." To what times of persecution can Sir Rider Haggard be referring, those of Diocletian, or those under Elizabeth? And if this hiding-place was constructed under Elizabeth, how on earth did the walled-up nuns come there? However, "opening out of this crypt is a darksome hole, where—so

I learned locally, and the person who showed me over the place stated—the skeletons and the pitcher were found by workmen who broke through the wall while executing repairs to the fabric. Of course it may be that the tale is false, and no such skeletons were found." Thus far Sir Rider Haggard. And I will venture to add: It may also be that the skeletons were not those of nuns and were never intentionally walled-up. Further investigation, indeed, makes it clear that there is not a scrap of evidence to suggest that the remains are those of nuns. The house is at Cheshunt it appears, and nearly two miles from Waltham Cross. Part of the basement *may* be older than the reign of Henry VIII, but it is not suggested that these foundations ever formed part of a religious house of any kind.[1]

It may be added that a few years ago a question was printed in *Notes and Queries*[2] asking for justification for the belief that apostate nuns were walled-up alive. Among all the collectors of out-of-the-way information who contribute to that periodical, only one answer was sent in, and this consisted in nothing more than a reference to the familiar Coldingham story. Six months later the same correspondent sent a quotation from Lord Malmesbury's *Memoirs,* from which it appeared that some mummified remains had been seen by Lord Malmesbury in "the Church at Arezzo," which he believed to be those of a man who had been walled-up alive.[3] With regard to this, I will content myself with remarking that one would hardly expect immured monks to be exposed for inspection in a cathedral, while, on the other hand, there are

---

[1] See Walford's *Greater London,* vol. i. p. 387.

[2] January, 1886. *Notes and Queries,* 7th Series, vol. i. p. 48.

[3] Vol. i. p. 181, see *Notes and Queries,* July 10th, 1886. Lord Malmesbury says nothing about the remains being those of a *monk,* but the correspondent who sends the quotation of course takes that for granted.

well-known instances of desiccated bodies being left open to view in that way—the corpse (*salma*)[1] of Estore, or Astore Visconti, who was killed in a duel in 1413, still standing upright in the churchyard wall beside the Cathedral of Monza, is a case in point.

Before leaving this subject I am glad to point out that in the 1896 edition of *Montezuma's Daughter* the statement of fact regarding the Mexican mummy was withdrawn, and is no longer vouched for by the author as sober matter of history. In removing the offending footnote from the place which it formerly occupied, Sir Rider Haggard has referred to the change in a brief Preface, chiefly remarkable for its scientific caution. In consequence, he tells us, of the disputes to which it has given rise, "the author withdraws the note, and expresses his regret that, in all good faith, he should have set down as fact that which has been proved to be a matter of controversy."

Well! there are some people, no doubt, to whom the story of Pope Joan or the Ptolemaic system of astronomy are still only matters of controversy. The controversy in this case lies between the officials of the Museum, the President of the Mexican Academy, and all the scholars of the country, on the one hand, and, on the other, a few dissenting Protestant missionaries, who are equally prepared to assert that nuns are poisoned and walled-up in English convents at the present day.

Still, despite the somewhat grudging tone of this concession, we must respect the feeling which prompted the author to make it, just as we unreservedly accept his statement that the note was originally written in good faith. Be it remarked, however, at the same time that attention has been directed here to one only of Sir Rider Haggard's misrepresentations of Catholic practice. It must not be supposed that no others are to be found in his novel. The

---

[1] See Amati, *Dizionario Corografico dell' Italia,* vol. v, p. 430. A modern traveller describes these remains as a sort of natural mummy.

statement of the abbess, quoted on page 4, who "has her pardon under seal," for a crime which she is about to commit, but has not committed, is an even more serious libel upon the creed of Catholics. But it is impossible to deal with it here.

One last word. Sir Rider Haggard complains of the folly of "raising so much dust" over things which are supposed to have happened three hundred years ago. It is his own allies in the campaign who supply the answer. One is glad that he has committed himself in print to the statement that "the horrors formerly perpetrated in the name of religion, not by one party but by all, are happily done with now" (letter of August 9th); but any one who read the correspondence would have seen that that was not the idea of Sir Rider Haggard's supporters. For them these things are going on in convents still. The bodies walled up in Mexico belong to the middle of the last century: bodies were found freshly buried alive in Parisian churches in 1871. Sir Rider Haggard's novel will still be quoted by these gentlemen as a true picture of religious life as it was and *is,* just as his footnote was held to endorse, from his own personal observation, the stories of wholesale poisoning told by "escaped nuns" all over the country.

THE IMMURING OF NUNS

BY THE REV. HERBERT THURSTON, S.J.

> And now the blind old Abbot rose
> To speak the Chapter's doom
> On those the wall was to enclose
> Alive within the tomb.
> (Scott, *Marmion*, canto ii. 25.)

AMONG the treasured convictions which have sunk deep down into the heart of the ordinary English Protestant, there is none more firmly rooted than the belief that all monasteries, but more especially the houses of religious women, are essentially prisons. In a moment of weakness, despondency, or highly wrought enthusiasm (disappointed love seems to be held responsible by the class of persons to whom we refer for about 90 per cent. of vocations to the cloister), the poor deluded victim takes the fatal step and gives in her name to a religious order. From that hour she is bound by adamantine chains. In a more primitive state of society, we are told, the natural result of this system was to lead to grave moral disorders, to convert tender women into cruel fanatics, or at least to destroy in them all independent judgment even of right and wrong. But in some cases the prisoner driven to desperation will break out into open revolt. When this took place, the well-instructed Protestant knows exactly what followed. A solemn conclave was held, the nun who had transgressed her vows was compelled to undergo some terrible imprisonment or torture, and in extreme cases amid a mockery of religious ceremonial she was built up alive into a niche in the wall to perish slowly by hunger and suffocation.

No one can suspect a man like Sir Walter Scott of pandering to mere vulgar bigotry, and yet this is the legend for which he pledges his credit as a student of history in a well-known episode of *Marmion*. Since his day this monstrous fiction may have fallen a little lower in the scale of respectability, but it is very far from having died out. There is hardly an anti-Catholic meeting of any kind, at which, if the question of convent life happens to turn up, the old charge is not in some shape or other repeated. When the Birmingham Oratory was in course of erection, as readers of Cardinal Newman's *Present Position of Catholics* will remember, something very like a popular outbreak took place excited by the discovery of a supposed series of dungeons in the basement. Still more recently a similar calumny was circulated among the Protestant workmen at Stonyhurst during the first stages of the erection of a ventilating shaft. But to illustrate the shape in which this venerable spectre is continually being resuscitated, I cannot do better than quote a passage from a lecture on *Convents Romish and Anglican* printed only a few months back, and prepared as a handbook to accompany a set of magic-lantern slides. The entertainment thus provided is intended, it seems, for Young Men's Societies and Sunday Schools, and is to be introduced, be it understood, *by prayer.*

"But we have yet another punishment that is probably still in use in the Romish system, and that is burying the nun alive. It is almost incredible that Satan can exercise such power over men as to make them believe it is right to do this. It is probably borrowed in part from the ancient custom of burying alive the vestal virgin who had committed some crime. In Mexico, owing to the climate, most perfect skeletons of walled-up nuns have lately been discovered in a state of complete preservation in old disused monasteries. Here is a picture of one. Dr. Grattan Guinness has seen such skeletons there quite lately."[1]

To illustrate this we have "Slide 30, *Walling up a Nun,*" "Slide 31, *Skeleton of Immured Nun.*"

Gross as is the calumny involved in a charge like this, it is not always, as some of my readers may have had occasion to discover, the easiest thing in the world to refute it satisfactorily.[2] The majority of the writers who repeat such statements do not think it necessary to refer to any definite instances in support of their assertions. Of those who make a pretence of proof the greater number confine themselves to examples located in far-off countries, or dependent upon the testimony of persons whose evidence cannot for various reasons be subjected to any examination. There remain, however, a few instances which seem more or less within range, and as these are appealed to with all confidence by the more respectable of the assailants of monastic life, there can be no injustice in taking them as test cases to see the value of the evidence upon which the charges rest. This is what I have tried to do in the pages which follow, and the reader must judge of the results for himself. Space is precious in a pamphlet like the present, so waiving further preamble let us address ourselves at once to the task before us. We may take for our first example a case which illustrates well the spirit in which the inquiry is approached by writers on the other side.

In a work called the *History of the Inquisition,*[3] by W. H. Rule, D.D., there is given at some length an account of the case of Fra Tominaso di Mileto, a conventual friar of the Order of St.

---

[1] Church Association and National Protestant League. Lecture No. 4, *Convents Romish and Anglican.* By the Rev. W. L. Holland, M.A.

[2] Few Catholic writers, it would seem, have thought it worth while to discuss the question seriously. There is an excellent article, however, on the subject by Mr. Edward Peacock, F.S.A., in the *Dublin Review* for January, 1889.

[3] Second Edit. Two Vols. London, 1874.

Francis and a "victim" of the Roman Inquisition. The narrative, as Dr. Rule explains, is based upon some authentic records of the Holy Office which have curiously enough found their way into the library of Trinity College, Dublin.[1] Friar Tommaso has been found guilty of maintaining certain heretical propositions, denying, among other matters, the doctrine of the Real Presence and the Sacrament of Penance. Final judgment in the case was pronounced by Cardinal [St. Charles] Borromeo, who sentenced the offender to be "deprived of all ecclesiastical dignities and honours," but inasmuch as he was penitent "absolved him from the censures thus pronounced and ordered that he should receive absolution at once, under condition of returning to the Church and doing penance, the form of which penance is described in every particular, including the *abitello,* or penitential habit with a cross." Dr. Rule then continues: "This, it might have been thought, would have been accounted sufficient for a forgiven penitent, but after it comes the following dreadful sentence, necessary to satisfy the anger of the Church:

"'And because it is not convenient and just to be zealous only in taking vengeance for offences committed against princes of the world, and yet not to be concerned for offences committed against the Divine Majesty, and also that crimes may not remain unpunished with bad example to our neighbour, it is our pleasure that you be walled up in a place surrounded with four walls—*che tu sij murato in un loco circondato da quattro mura*—which place we will cause to be assigned to you; where with anguish of heart and abundance of tears, you shall bewail your sins and offences committed against the majesty of God, the holy mother Church,

---

[1] I see no reason to doubt the genuineness of these documents. See the paper by K. Benrath in Von Sybel's *Historische Zeitschrift,* 1879, i. p. 254. Cf. the articles by the same writer in the *Allgemeine Zeitung* for 1877, and in the *Rivista Cristiana* of Florence for 1880.

and the religion of the Father St. Francis, in which you have made profession.'"

And here we may pause for a moment before we allow Dr. Rule to express the emotions with which these horrors have filled him. It should, we might think, have occurred to him that he had possibly misconceived the meaning of the original text. The word *murato,* as any fairly good dictionary will show, does not necessarily mean *walled up* in Italian, any more than the word "immured" necessarily means *walled up* in English.[1] The sentence enjoins that the friar is to be "confined within four walls," until he has had time to think over his conduct and give reasonable assurance of future good behaviour. This is the natural meaning of the words; the more so as the substantive *murus* in mediaeval Latin and all the derivative tongues was very commonly used in the sense of "prison." Moreover, it is borne out by an appeal to any dictionary of authority, like, the great work of Tommaseo, as well as by the fact that the phrase "within four walls"[2] is more or less idiomatic in every European language. The only thing "dreadful" in this matter is the intensity of the prejudice which, against all antecedent probability, jumps at once at the unfavourable interpretation. But we are interrupting the stream of Dr. Rule's indignant pathos. He thus continues: "So within four walls built up around him, but with sufficient space to kneel down before a crucifix and an image of the Virgin, this poor man was to be confined, and out of that place he was not to stir, but there suffer anguish of heart,

---

[1] See, e.g., any recent edition of Baretti, where under the word *murare,* we have "to inclose, shut in."

[2] The phrase, *tra quattro mura,* is used of any close confinement without free egress, and Tommaseo with his liberalist prejudices cites the phrase, *chiudere tra quattro mura una fanciulla,* as a popular equivalent of sending a girl into a convent. But even Dr. Rule will hardly suppose that every girl that goes into a convent is *walled-up.* Cf. the French *mettre entre quatre murailles.*

and shed many tears. There was no order given for any door, but
only four walls were to be built up around him; and from what
we know of these structures, we may suppose that a small opening
was to be left above, for food to be dropped down to him. It was
what would be called in England 'a little-ease,' where the prisoner
was to be kept to putrify and expire in his own filth."[1]

The reference at this point to the "little-ease" of dear old
England was perhaps slightly infelicitous, and Dr. Rule seems to
have had his attention called to the slip. Accordingly in the later
edition[2] he is careful to guide the minds of his readers into the
proper channel by the addition of the words (little-ease) "in the
days of Bonner." It is to be hoped that all right-minded Anglicans
perusing this passage will fix their attention carefully in future
upon the tyrannies of Bloody Mary, and not allow their thoughts
to stray by any chance distraction in the direction of our good
Queen Bess. But it is rather unfortunate that while the torture
of the "little-ease" meets the student at every turn during the
persecutions under Elizabeth, it is hardly known to have been
used in the time of her elder sister. Finally, after a reference to
some human remains seen by a Mr. Witherell in the walls of the
Inquisition at Seville, Dr. Rule concludes in evident bewilderment:
"By some means or other, Fra Tommaso, the Minorite, escaped
from his 'place with four walls.' He might have found a loose stone
in the wall and broken through, or some one of the servants may
have pitied him, and helped him to get out. Be that as it might,
his effigy was burnt, according to a sentence read on the 8th of
November, 1565."

Perhaps it is hardly necessary to take Dr. Rule quite seriously
in all this, but it may be worth while to call attention to two significant facts which do not certainly make in favour of his view of

---

[1] *History of the Inquisition*, First Edit. p. 375.
[2] *Ib*. Second Edit. vol. ii. p. 197.

a Roman "immuring." In the year 1578, that is a little more than twelve years after the events here described, there was printed in Rome an edition of Eymeric's *Directorium Inquisitorum*, with a new commentary by Francis Pegna, a learned canonist who had long been connected with the Holy Office both in that city and in Spain. The book was issued to serve as a *manual of procedure for the Inquisitors themselves.* It was dedicated to Pope Gregory XIII. and appeared with all sorts of official sanctions. In this work Pegna commenting upon the term *immuratio* which occurs in Eymeric's text, declares that "the punishment of immuring is altogether the same as that of perpetual confinement in a public gaol, contrary to what some people suppose who are ignorant of the antiquity of the latter institution."[1] No doubt Dr. Rule would find no difficulty in believing that this statement was sanctioned by the Roman Inquisitors at the very time that a score of prisoners were still pining away in walled-up niches within a dozen yards of them. But those who understand the nature of Pegna's work will not be able to accept this explanation. The second fact lies in a detail of the sentence passed on Fra Tommaso and others similarly condemned to be *murati.* He was to receive the Blessed Eucharist, if his confessor approved, once a week. Was this also "to be dropped down to him from a small opening left above"? Catholics will not readily suppose that St. Charles Borromeo in passing sentence can have contemplated that.

But let us suppose that Dr. Rule, and the author from whom he borrows, are perfectly correct in their interpretations—what,

---

[1] F. Pegna, *Annotationes in Directorium Inquisitorum Eymerici,* p. 184, Romæ, 1578: "Eandem prorsus esse poenam immurationis et carceris perpetui, contra quam quidam hujus antiquitatis ignari censeant." It would seem from some sentences of the Inquisition, published by Benrath in the *Rivista Cristiana,* that *carcer perpetuus* is to be understood rather of the place than of the punishment.

we may ask, would follow? Let us suppose that Fra Tommaso was really condemned, as they seem to imagine, to stand patiently in an open space while the stone-masons of the Holy Office solemnly erected four walls around him—what is the peculiar horror of this form of imprisonment? After all he was to receive his daily rations, he had room enough to turn round in, with "a crucifix and a statue of the Virgin," and as the event showed, he was not debarred from the hope of escape. This is a totally different thing from the ordinary Protestant conception of nuns built up alive into a niche in the wall to starve or to suffocate in a few hours. Heaven forbid that we should seek to extenuate the horrors of any form of perpetual imprisonment in one spot, but whether the sufferer was shut in by masonry or by a door whose bolts were never to be drawn back, could hardly make so very much difference. Yet at that epoch there was scarcely a castle or civil prison in Europe but had dungeons where victims might be and were immured until death came to deliver them. It is shocking and terrible to look back upon, no doubt, but it is no more reasonable to seek to create a prejudice against Catholics on that score, than it would be to condemn the British nation of immodesty because their ancestors went naked.

Now it is precisely this sort of evidence which is largely appealed to in a vague and ill-defined way to support the calumny of the immuring of nuns. In the conception of Sir Walter Scott, and in the mouths of those who shelter themselves behind his authority, a plain and clear charge is made that nuns who broke their vows were not uncommonly built up into niches in the wall. Mrs. Browning, in her *Lay of the Brown Rosary*, uses language that is equally unmistakable:

> A nun in the east wall was buried alive,
> Who mocked at the priest when he called her to shrive,
> And shrieked such a curse, *as the stone took her breath,*

The old abbess fell backward and swooned unto death,
    With an *Ave* half-spoken.

Sir Walter is so well acquainted with the whole proceeding that he informs us in a note, which I shall have occasion to quote in full later on, that "the awful words *vade in pace* were the signal for immuring the criminal." Where he obtained his information he does not say; but this much happens to be true, that the phrase *in pace* is used in modern French as a synonym for dungeon or *cachot*,[1] and is applied more or less technically by archæologists to the prison-cells found in some ancient monasteries for the confinement of refractory religious. These cells were in no sense niches in the wall such as Sir Walter Scott has in mind, neither were they walled up, but they were closed with doors like other cells, barred no doubt from the outside by those in charge of the prisoner. That they were often the reverse of luxurious, needs no saying, for they were intended for the punishment of those whose ordinary conditions of life as to food, clothing, and lodging would be regarded with horror by the inmate of a modern convict prison. What the history of the word *in pace* as applied to these structures has been, I have found it impossible to ascertain satisfactorily.[2] The word has been used in French since the sixteenth century or earlier, but in Latin Ducange offers but a single example, and that under the heading *vade in pace*. Strange to say, it is always to this same example that any modern writers who happen to give references lead us back either mediately or immediately, until the doubt arises whether the use of the phrase for a monastic prison-cell was

---

[1]   Il faudrait
    Dit l'infant Ruy, trouver quelque couvent discret
    Quelqu' *in pace* bien calme où cet enfant vieillisse.
                         (Victor Hugo, *Ruy Blas*.)
[2] Little or nothing is to be found on the subject in Littré, Bescherelle, Ducange, Godefroy, or Scheler.

ever anything more than a local designation in mediæval times, arising possibly in the grim humour of one particular monastery. However, this is quite a subsidiary point. The important fact is, that when the phrase *in pace* is used by continental writers, or when an appeal is made to history to illustrate its meaning, we find that the instances given are simply cases of perpetual imprisonment, and in no instance have the slightest reference to walling-up alive in the sense of Sir Walter Scott. Of course it is impossible to speak quite positively in such a matter. The difficulty of proving a negative is proverbial, and he would be a rash man who would venture to set a limit to the horrors which a mediæval controversialist in a rage was capable of laying to the charge of his adversaries. But this much may be said, that after examining such few references as are quoted by those who declare that the practice of walling-up alive was a fact, I have not yet come across an instance where there was the least reason to suppose that the writer was thinking of the bricking up of a niche in the sense of Scott's *Marmion.* Cases occur undoubtedly of confinement in some cruelly narrow cell. More than once the accusation is made that prisoners were deliberately allowed to starve upon a pittance insufficient to support life. But these instances are all quite different from the "living tomb" of the poet, the idea uppermost in the minds of the lecturers and platform orators who make capital of it to excite the horror of their audience.

For the majority of these gentlemen it is impossible, for reasons already explained, to submit their statements to any investigation; but we may examine, as far as space will permit, the allegations made by some of the more respectable of those who disseminate the tradition. From these we may learn how little to expect of the others.

An American writer, a Mr. H. C. Lea, who enjoys among his own countrymen a considerable reputation for historical research, has published of late years three substantial volumes entitled *A*

History of the Inquisition of the Middle Ages. The author has apparently spent his life[1] in raking together with laborious assiduity every scandal and every gruesome story he could find which reflected unfavourably upon the mediæval Church in any part of the world. "The evil that men do lives after them" we are told on good authority, and the natural result of this accumulation of horrors unrelieved by any attempt to examine the brighter colours of the picture has been to produce in Mr. Lea's mind an extremely strong bias against the Catholic Church in the fourteenth and fifteenth centuries. At the same time Mr. Lea is a writer of quite a different stamp from some of the fanatics referred to above. He is an educated man who understands the value of documentary evidence, and who would not, I am fain to believe, be guilty of any intentional falsification of his materials. Naturally Mr. Lea has been led to devote a good deal of attention to the religious punishments of the middle ages, and one turns with considerable interest to his pages, feeling sure that any horror or cruelty in monasteries or out of them, for which evidence can be quoted, will not have escaped his diligence. What adds to the importance of his work is the fact that he has incorporated in it all the researches of M. Molinier of Toulouse, who has devoted many years to investigating the MS. records of the Inquisition in the South of France,[2] a region where the cruelties practised against the Albigensian and Waldensian heretics have long supplied Protestant controversialists with a favourite topic of declamation.

That Mr. Lea has plenty to tell about the various forms of imprisonment enjoined by the Inquisition need hardly be said. The technical name for it, at any rate in the South of France, was *murus,* a fact which may be commended to the consideration of our friend Dr. Rule; it was divided into three kinds, *largus, strictus,*

---

[1] I refer here particularly to the *History of Celibacy* by the same author.
[2] Molinier, *L'Inquisition dans le Midi de la France.*

and *strictissimus.* In the case of the *murus largus,* the prisoner was allowed to take exercise in the corridors; in the *strictus,* he was not allowed to leave his cell; in the *murus strictissimus,*[1] he was thrust into some dreadful dungeon, chained, it would seem, hand and foot.[2] It does not appear that the regulations were always enforced with equal severity, and M. Molinier gives numerous instances of the prisoners obtaining *licentiam exeundi murum*—leave to quit the precincts of the gaol, sometimes for six weeks or more together.

It is important to call attention to the meaning here given to *murus,* because the word seems to have led even some Catholic writers into the belief—as I conceive, an erroneous one—that the offenders condemned to perpetual prison had the door of their cells literally *walled up,* though apertures were left both for light and for the introduction of food. Now Eymeric, himself Inquisitor General, the author of the official handbook of inquisitorial procedure, says in this work: "In some towns, as at Toulouse and at Carcassonne, the Inquisitors have in their establishment prisons, which they call *muri,* because these cells are contiguous to the *walls of the town.*"[3] If this etymology be correct, it has a curious analogy to that of the *piombi* of Venice—the dungeons underneath *the leads,* in which Silvio Pellico, for instance, was confined. But however the name arose, Messrs. Lea and Molinier would be the first to confess that for Eymeric and for other writers of that epoch

---

[1] The *murus strictissimus* is mentioned by Mr. Lea. M. Molinier, the more trustworthy investigator, speaks only of *murus largus* and *murus strictus.*

[2] The stench and filth of some of the Elizabethan prisons, of which we have details too horrible to be set down here, exceed anything recorded of the dungeons of the Inquisition. See, *e.g.,* Father Pollen's *Acts of English Martyrs* or Jardine's *Use of Torture,* &c. We may notice also an interesting parallel to the *murus largus* and *strictus* in the "liberty of gaol" and "close prison" of which we have record in the same reign.

[3] See *Directorium Inquisitorum,* p. 635.

no blocking up with masonry was implied by the word *immuratio*. That Pegna, a sort of consultor to the Inquisition, and a man who had every means of knowing the truth, wrote in the same sense in Rome three centuries later, we have already seen.

Of course in many cases there was a severity shown which no one could attempt to excuse, except on the ground that it was absolutely universal at that epoch, and lasted, in our own country for instance, until long after Reformation times. On the sufferings of the victim, as might be expected, Mr. Lea dilates with gusto. But if anybody should search his volumes for confirmation of the legend supported by Sir Walter Scott he will meet very little to reward his pains.

One instance, however, to which he refers has some bearing upon the matter in question, and may be quoted here. Religious, Mr. Lea tells us, convicted of heresy were not confined in the prisons of the Inquisition but in the cells provided in the different monasteries for the punishment of offenders. "In the case of Jeanne, widow of B. de la Tour, a nun of Lespinasse, in 1246, who had committed acts of both Catharan and Waldensian heresy, and had prevaricated in her confession, the sentence was confinement in a separate cell in her own convent, where no one was to enter or see her, her food being pushed in through an opening left for the purpose, in fact the living tomb known as the *in pace.*"[1]

It need hardly be remarked that this case is very far from bearing out the notion of the *in pace* which is found in Sir Walter Scott. There is not a word about walling up, and it is quite clear that the

---

[1] Lea, op. cit. i. p. 487. It may be worth while to remark that as far as I have been able to examine the abundant Inquisition literature published of late years by Douais, Fredericq, Molinier, Clæssens, Medina, Henner, and others, no attempt is now made by serious students to substantiate against the Inquisition the charge of walling up its prisoners alive.

prisoner was supplied with food. But it is particularly interesting because from the prominence given to it both by Mr. Lea and M. Molinier, it is tolerably clear that they have no instance to adduce of greater severity.

But Mr. Lea adds in a note: "The cruelty of the monastic system of imprisonment known as *in pace*, or *vade in pacem*, was such that those subjected to it speedily died in all the agonies of despair," and then he goes on to cite the appeal of the Archbishop of Toulouse to King John of France to mitigate the severity of this solitary confinement, and the resulting *ordonnance* of the King that the Superior of the convent should twice a month visit and console the prisoner, who moreover should have the right twice a month to ask for the company of one of the monks.[1] Now it is a curious fact that the one passage here referred to is the only justification I have been able to find of the use of the word *in pace* by mediæval writers in the sense of prison. As already mentioned, Ducange gives only this solitary example, and writers after quoting from one another seem always in the end to be traceable to this. It is fortunate however that the letter defines the meaning of the term so that we can see how little it accords with the modern conception. This cruel imprisonment which is called by the monks *vade in pace,* is explained by the merciful Archbishop to be perpetual and solitary confinement in a gloomy dungeon upon bread and water, and he asks the Sovereign to insist upon its mitigation, as it is found that many sufferers die under it. Strict orders for its alleviation, as already mentioned, were at once issued by King

---

[1] The document is given at length in Baluze's notes to *Capitularia Regum Francorum*, ii. p. 1088. A story sometimes quoted (*e.g.* by Mabillon, *Ouvrages Posthumes* ii. p. 323), from the *Liber Miraculorum* of Peter of Clugny (ii. 9) about a monk who was buried alive in the ground, seems to me to describe only a device adopted to frighten an impenitent offender, not a punishment seriously persisted in.

John, and indeed there may be found in the Canonists reference to more than one ordinance of the Holy See passing restrictions upon the too great severity of the monastic prisons. To enter into these would take us too far from our present purpose, but it may be sufficient to repeat that neither here nor in the revelations of Messrs. Lea and Molinier is there any suggestion to be found of walled-up niches or of the withdrawal of that modicum at least of bread and water, necessary to sustain life.[1] Such regulations as we do find enjoining the occasional companionship of other monks seem on the contrary to point to a cell that could be entered by a door or at least to one that permitted easy communication with the outside world.[2]

Somewhat nearly akin to these punishment cells which the

---

[1] Compare with this treatment the *peine forte et dure* of English Common Law enacted against the prisoner who stood "mute of malice." He was to be "stretched upon his back and to have iron laid upon him as much as he could bear and more, and so to continue, fed upon bad bread and stagnant water, through alternate days until he pleaded or died." (Stephen, *History of the Criminal Law*, i. p. 297.) It was last inflicted as recently as the year 1726.

[2] One or two other details may be added. Mr. Lea says: "While the penance prescribed was a diet of bread and water, the Inquisition, with unwonted kindness, did not object to its prisoners receiving from their friends contributions of food, wine, money, and garments, and among its documents are such frequent allusions to this that it may be regarded as an established custom." (p. 491.) Again the same writer complains "that *through long years* the miserable inmates endured a living death far worse than the short agony of the stake." We need not stay to inquire whether perpetual imprisonment is worse than death, but it is clear that the prisoners *lived*, which is not the idea of Exeter Hall. Lastly, it is also beyond question, from the evidence both of Molinier and Mr. Lea, that the Holy See from time to time intervened peremptorily on the side of mercy. In 1306, under Clement V., the Inquisitor, a bishop, was deposed.

French call *in pace's*, and in the delightfully vague language of
anti-Popery declamation commonly identified with them, is the
oubliette. Properly speaking the *oubliette* should be regarded as the
adjunct of the feudal castle rather than of the mediæval monastery.
By archæologists, who are accurate in the use of terms, the word
is used to denote a sort of well or secret chamber constructed
under the floor of a room, and so arranged that the victim whom
it was desired to get rid of could be precipitated into it through a
trapdoor or other contrivance. There he was killed by the fall or
left to starve. Now, as it cannot be too often repeated, this paper
by no means undertakes the defence of mediæval punishments,
but still it is worth while pointing out how utterly unreliable in
their regard is the voice of popular tradition, and I venture to
quote on the subject of the *oubliette* a few words from M. Viollet
le Duc, an archæologist whose acquaintance with the byways of
mediæval architecture is confessedly unrivalled. There is hardly
an ancient castle, says this authority[1] whose words I am forced
to condense, where the attention of the visitor is not called to
the *oubliettes*, but the vast majority of the pits so designated are
nothing more nor less than latrines. I have seen, he continues, in
plenty of castles, abbeys, and other ancient buildings, dungeons
(*des cachots*), and punishment cells (*des vade in pace*), but I know
only three *oubliettes* which have any claim to be considered as
such. Of these three the only one as to whose destination he is
satisfied is that of the Castle of Pierrefonds. M. Viollet le Duc had
himself lowered to the bottom of the shaft, but no trace whatever existed of any human remains, although no visible means
of removing them existed if any one had ever been precipitated
there. Altogether upon the whole question M. Viollet le Duc finds
himself in entire agreement with the hardly less distinguished

---

[1] *Dictionnaire Raisonné de l'Architecture Française au Moyen Age*, vol.
vi. pp. 452, 453.

archæologist, M. Prosper Mérimée, whose words he quotes. "The middle ages are too often painted in extravagant colours, and the imagination accepts much too readily the atrocities which romance writers assign to spots like these. How many wine vaults and wood cellars have been mistaken for frightful dungeons! How many bones thrown away from the kitchen have been regarded as the remains of the victims of feudal tyranny!" He then instances the case of these *oubliettes* and concludes: "Without absolutely denying the existence of such things, they ought nevertheless to be considered as very rare and only to be admitted where there is clear proof of the purpose they were intended to serve."[1] As for the walled-up niche which is in question here, I know only one archæologist of repute[2] who has taken the trouble to investigate the matter seriously. The verdict of this Anglican Archdeacon is that "there never was a time when such things could have been true." For the rest the more respectable writers are content with an appeal to the authority of Sir Walter Scott, or a vague reference to certain "discoveries" which are not found upon examination to rest upon very reliable evidence. I propose to devote the remainder of this paper to the investigation of some of these stories.

When Sir Walter Scott introduced into *Marmion* the episode so often referred to, he added at the same time a note which may as well be given entire: "It is well known that the religious who broke their vows of chastity were subjected to the same penalty as the Roman vestals in a similar case. A small niche, sufficient to enclose their bodies, was made in the massive wall of the convent;

---

[1] *Instructions du Comité historique des arts et momuments,—Architecture Militaire*, pp. 75–82.

[2] Archdeacon Churton in his paper on *Penitential Cells and Prisons* connected with Monastic Houses, read before the Yorkshire Architectural Society and printed in Associated Architectural Societies Reports, vol. ii. p. 219. I am indebted to Mr. Peacock's article for the reference.

a slender pittance of food and water was deposited in it, and the awful words, *Vade in pace,* were the signal for immuring the criminal. It is not likely that in latter times this punishment was often resorted to; but among the ruins of the Abbey of Coldingham, were some years ago discovered the remains of a female skeleton, which from the shape of the niche and the position of the figure, seemed to be that of an immured nun." (Note 2 M.) To which Lockhart in his edition of the poems adds this valuable comment: "The Edinburgh Reviewer, on stanza xxxii. *post,* suggests that the proper reading of the sentence is *vade in pacem*— not *part in peace,* but *go into peace,* or into eternal rest, a pretty intelligible *mittimus* to another world."

It is a pity that Sir Walter Scott has not made us acquainted with the sources whence he derived this important information. The reference to Coldingham, however, is at least something to go upon, although even that might certainly be more definite. Still Coldingham is not unknown to fame. As early as the beginning of the seventh century, St. Ebba, or Abb, built a nunnery there, which seems to have been of the kind called mixed—*i.e.,* including both monks and nuns under the rule of an Abbess. It was destroyed by the Danes before 880, but in 1098 a priory for monks was founded in the same spot by Edgar, King of Scotland, as an appanage to Durham. In this way Coldingham comes to occupy a very considerable place in Raine's great *History of North Durham.* It receives full attention also in Mackenzie Walcott's *Ancient Church of Scotland,* as well as in Chalmers' *Caledonia,* Ridpath's *Border History,* and many other works, so that it seemed not unreasonable to expect that from one source or another satisfactory details would be forthcoming about Sir Walter Scott's immured nun. To detail the various incidents of the quest undertaken in pursuit of this *ignis fatuus* would be highly uninteresting.[1] In the majority of

---

[1] It may be worth while to mention that a letter addressed to the min-

the authoritative works named, and in a number of others, there is no allusion whatever to the discovery. On the other hand, the compilers of modern guide-books mention the episode to a man, copying each other, but of course without references. It will be sufficient therefore to say that the earliest mention of the story I have been able to find occurs in Grose's *Antiquities of Scotland* (1789), in the following words: "Some years ago in taking down a tower at the south-west corner of the building, a skeleton of a woman was found, who from several circumstances appeared to have been immured. She had her shoes on, which were long preserved in the custody of the minister."[1]

It is perhaps not too much to infer from this notice that the discovery must have been made a considerable time before Mr. Grose wrote. The remark that "her shoes were long preserved in the custody of the minister," seems rather to imply that they had then disappeared, and the mention of "a tower in the south-west corner of the building," leaves us to choose between two alternatives, either that the discovery was made in a wing of the priory where it cannot be pretended that nuns ever lived, as the priory was built solely for men, or that the date of the find was so remote that some of St. Ebba's nunnery was still standing. It is probably for this reason that Mr. Grose, a careful antiquary, says nothing about *nuns* or *in pace's,* but speaks only of "a woman who seemed to have been immured." Somewhat fuller details are given by later writers, but for brevity's sake we may content ourselves with the account to be found in Carr's *History of Coldingham,* still the standard work on the locality, composed in 1836 by a resident antiquary who was also a medical man: "On removing a portion

---

ister of Coldingham asking if he could kindly supply any details or any references to a contemporary account of the discovery, has met with no reply.

[1] F. Grose, *Antiquities of Scotland* (1789), p. 95.

of the ruins about fifty years ago, the bones of a female skeleton were discovered enclosed in a niche in one of the walls, which from its position, and the narrowness of the depository, are supposed to have been the remains of an *immured nun*. ... Two sandals of thin leather, furnished with latchets of silk, were also found lying at the bottom of the recess.[1] Could it be satisfactorily proved that the skeleton was actually that of a nun, all doubt respecting the site of the last of the double monasteries would be dispelled, for as the priory was devoted exclusively to monks, the body must necessarily have been deposited there previous to its erection. In the absence of such evidence, it may be questioned whether it may not have been the remains of a monk who had been buried in an upright posture; there being on record several instances of such a mode of burial practised in the Benedictine monasteries."[2]

Three extremely interesting conclusions may be deduced from the latter portion of this account. In the first place we learn that the site even of the original nunnery of St. Ebb is a matter of conjecture. Strange to say, the argument is not, as we might expect—a skeleton has been found among ruins known to be those of an ancient nunnery, therefore the skeleton is that of a nun. But it runs *ex converso*—human remains are found apparently walled up in a ruin, therefore the ruin must be that of a house of religious women.

Secondly we are reminded, that as the nunnery was finally wrecked by the Danes in 875, the remains, if those of one of the inmates, must have been in the wall for more than nine hundred years, which is a long time for the sandals to have been perfectly preserved in a situation so dubiously air-tight. I say nothing of the fact that the nunnery was destroyed by fire, which might have

---

[1] "The sandals were long in the possession of the late Mr. Johnston, factor to the estate of Billy." (Note by Dr. Carr.)

[2] A. A. Carr, *History of Coldingham Priory*, p. 316.

been supposed to shrivel the leather, even behind a wall.

Lastly, Dr. Carr lets us see that he, a diligent and competent investigator living on the spot, and therefore presumably able to question those with whom remained the tradition of the discovery, had found nothing to satisfy him that the remains were even those of a female.

A complaint was made a page or two back that no satisfactory particulars were forthcoming about this interesting find. Perhaps the reader will after all be disposed to think that the evidence is sufficient—sufficient, that is to say, to show how utterly untrustworthy are all the conclusions based upon it.

Amongst the works mentioned above as conspicuous by their silence respecting the immured nun of Coldingham is Mr. Mackenzie Walcott's *Ancient Church of Scotland.* That Mr. Walcott should not have bestowed even a footnote upon the nun in his full account of Coldingham Priory is remarkable—the more so that in an earlier work he shows himself a devout believer in the good old Protestant tradition. In his justly-esteemed *Dictionary of Sacred Archæology,* under the heading (monastic) "Prison," we find the following statements: "In all cases solitary confinement was practised, and in some cases the guilty were immured, after the pronunciation of the sentence, *Vade in pace*—'Go in peace.' At Thornton the skeleton of Abbot de Multon, *c.* 1445, with a candlestick, chair (*sic*) and table, was found built up within a recess of the wall; and a cell with a loop looking towards the high altar, remains at the Temple, in which William (*sic*) le Bachelor, Grand Preceptor of Ireland, died."

Here then are two other interesting examples which invite verification. They are placed by Mr. Walcott in the front rank presumably as being the most satisfactory and the nearest home. At the same time we may remark *en passant* that neither the one nor the other in the least realizes the idea of Sir Walter Scott or the Exeter Hallites. But let that pass. Mr. Walcott unfortunately does not condescend to give references for particular statements. Instead of that, three or four pages at the beginning of his volume are devoted to a general citation of authorities, a practice which is about as helpful to those who desire to check his accuracy as if he had said, "*Vide* MSS. at British Museum, *passim*." By a fortunate accident, however, an examination, among other sources, of the index to the *British Archæological Journal* suggested a reference to the volume for 1846, where, in an article by J. H. P(arker) on *Thornton Abbey*, it was easy to recognize the source of Walcott's inspiration on the subject of Walter Multon.

All that is known upon this head may be given in very brief space indeed. William Stukeley, an archæologist of the eighteenth century, published in 1721 a work called *Itinerarium Curiosum*, the purpose of which is sufficiently described by its sub-title—"an account of the antiquitys and remarkable curiositys in nature or art observed in travels thro' Great Britain." Passing in one of his journeys by Thornton Abbey in Lincolnshire, he gives a rapid description of it. I quote the sentence which precedes and follows that which concerns our present subject, to show the casual nature of the reference.

"Along the ditch within the gate are spacious rooms and stair-cases of good stone and ribwork arches. Upon taking down an old wall there, they found a man with a candlestick, table and book, who was supposed to have been immured. When you enter the spacious court, a walk of trees conducts you to the ruins of the church."[1]

Now this brief notice seems to be the only foundation of the story. Mr. Parker cites no other authority, as he almost certainly would have done if he had found anything more satisfactory. A search made in county histories, in the *Gentleman's Magazine* and archæological journals, has resulted in nothing further. So

---

[1] Stukeley, *Itinerarium Curiosum*, p. 95. First Edit.

we are left for this fact to the casual remark of a traveller at the beginning of the eighteenth century who does not imply even that he believed the story, or saw the chamber, or knew how many years before his time the discovery may have been made. A candlestick, a table, and a book seem rather curious adjuncts for an immured man, and are certainly not provided for in Sir Walter Scott's plan of operations. Amongst the thousand and one accidents that might account for the discovery of a skeleton under such circumstances, the suggestion that the remains were those of an Elizabethan priest forgotten in a hiding-place would at least have something more to say for itself than the theory of the wiseacres of Thornton.

But Messrs. Parker and Walcott are not only satisfied about the immuring, but they know that the victim was Walter de Multon, Abbot of Thornton in 1443. It appears that the compiler of a MS. history of the Abbey[1] writing about the year 1525, says that he had been unable to find any record of the death or place of burial of this particular abbot. Whence Mr. Parker concludes: "It is almost impossible to doubt that this significant passage has allusion to the fate of Walter Multon, who expiated his unrecorded offences by suffering that dire punishment, which, we have reason to believe, the secret and irresponsible monastic tribunals of the middle ages occasionally inflicted upon their erring brethren."[2]

It ought to be mentioned perhaps that according to Mr. Parker an old tradition exists in the place of an abbot having been immured there,[3] but we are not told by whom the tradition was

---

[1] MS. Tanner, 166.

[2] *The Archæological Journal*, ii. p. 593. The "significance" of the passage is probably due to Mr. Parker's manner of translating it. He does not give the original Latin.

[3] For the value of tradition in such matters see the story of the "bairns boäns" at Fountains Abbey, quoted by Mr. Peacock, p. 45. The bones in question, supposed by local tradition to be those of children put out

ascertained, nor given any reason to think that this is more than a confused popular recollection of the incident mentioned by Stukeley.[1]

The other instance of an immured prisoner which Mr. Walcott cites with all the air of appealing to an ascertained fact as certain as the accession of Queen Victoria, is the case of "William," he means Walter, le Bacheler, whose supposed cell may still be visited in the Temple Church, London. His authority in this case would seem to have been the tolerably well-known work of Mr. Addison, published in 1842. However this may be, Mr. Addison's presentation of the facts is so dramatic that it would be a pity not to allow him to tell the story.

"This dreary place of solitary confinement is formed within the wall of the church, and is only four feet, six inches long, and two feet, six inches wide, so that it would be impossible for a grown man to lie down with any degree of comfort within it. Two small

---

of the way by the monks as soon as they were born, were examined by competent medical authority and pronounced to be pigs'!

[1] In a recently published volume entitled *Bygone Lincolnshire*, by W. Andrews, we read: "The Abbot's house on the south is now occupied as a farm-house. In making the excavations was found a tomb inscribed, 'Roberti et Julia (*sic*) 1443,' and in a wall was found a skeleton with a table, a book, and a candlestick, supposed to be the remains of *Thomas de Gretham*, the fourteenth Abbot, who was immured (buried alive within a wall) for some crime or breach of monastic rule. The Annals of the Abbey are somewhat scanty, there being little known of its ecclesiastical or domestic history." (p. 146.). The author of the paper in which this passage occurs, Mr. Frederick Ross, F.R.H.S., in answer to my inquiries, has kindly informed me that he is indebted for this information to Timbs. (*Abbeys and Castles*, vol. i. p. 374.) This looks like an independent tradition; but further investigation reveals that it is nothing of the sort. Timbs. simply copies somebody who copies Parker, and Mr. Ross has blundered in reproducing Timbs.

apertures or loopholes, four feet high and nine inches wide, have been pierced through the walls to admit light and air. One of these apertures looks eastward into the body of the church, towards the spot where stood the high altar, in order that the prisoner might see and hear the performance of Divine Service, and the other looks southward into the Round, facing the west entrance of the church. The hinges and catch of a door, firmly attached to the doorway of this dreary prison, still remain, and at the bottom of the staircase, is a stone recess, or cupboard, where bread and water were placed for the prisoner."[1]

Mr. Addison then continues: "In this miserable cell were confined the refractory and disobedient brethren of the Temple, and those who were enjoined severe penance with solitary confinement. Its dark secrets have long since been buried in the silence of the tomb, but one sad tale of misery and horror connected with it has been brought to light.

"Several of the brethen of the Temple at London, who were examined before the Papal Inquisitors, tell us of the miserable death of Brother Walter le Bacheler, Knight, Grand Preceptor of Ireland, who, for disobedience to his superior, the Master of the Temple, was fettered and cast into prison, and there expired from the rigour and severity of his confinement. His dead body was taken out of the solitary cell in the Temple at morning's dawn, and was buried by Brother John de Stoke and Brother Radulph de Barton, in the middle of the court, between the church and the hall."

As Mr. Addison is good enough to tell us whence he has derived his information[2] we are able to satisfy ourselves that the facts here narrated are substantially accurate. Certainly the depositions of

---

[1] Addison, *The Temple Church*, p. 75.
[2] Wilkins' *Concilia*, vol. ii. Examination of the Templars, pp. 337, 346, 377, 384.

the Templars at their trial make it clear that Walter le Bacheler had been severely handled in prison (*et bene audivit quod aliquæ duritiæ fuerunt ipsi factæ* are the words of one witness[1]) and that he had been buried with somewhat suspicious secrecy. We may add from the same source[2] that his imprisonment had lasted eight weeks, and that he had received the Sacrament of Penance and probably Holy Communion before death. But will the reader be surprised to hear that there is not a syllable to connect Walter le Bacheler with the cell in the tower? That he was not *walled up* there is in any case obvious, the fastenings of the door still remain, and the body was carried out to be buried. But the idea that this cell inside the church was ever used for the restraint of unwilling prisoners *in extremis* is a mere conjecture which has against it all the probabilities. Was it intended that the groans of the miserable victim should mingle, through two open apertures, with the praises of God chanted below? Was it likely that he would be confined where his cries would reach the ears of every casual visitor that entered the church? Were they so considerate of his spiritual welfare as to provide that he should have the altar and the ceremonies of Holy Mass constantly under his eyes? What may have been the true destination of this cell, with its commanding view both of the round and the rectangular area which make up the Temple Church, I cannot pretend to say for certain. It remains yet to be proved that it was meant for anything less innocent than a closet to keep brooms in. Possibly it might have been used by a voluntary recluse who was willing, in expiation of some crime, to undergo this unusually severe penance. The outlook upon the high altar is a feature which it has in common with the ordinary anchoret's cell, but of course its dimensions are much smaller

---

[1] *Ibid.* p. 337.
[2] *Ibid.* p. 346.

than the *reclusoria* of which we have examples.[1] On the whole the probabilities are greatly in favour of the opinion of Father Morris, F.S.A., who was kind enough to accompany me in a visit to the Temple Church. He pronounces confidently that it is nothing but a watching-loft (*excubitorium*) from which one of the brethren unobserved could command the high altar, the round, and indeed the whole building. In the cases of churches with shrines such constructions, though often of much larger dimensions, are very common,[2] and there seems to be some ground for thinking that they were not confined to noted places of pilgrimage, but may have existed also in other churches where there was no shrine.[3] In any case Mr. Addison has not a fragment of evidence or analogy to produce for his view, and yet he goes so far as to include in his book a sensational full-page engraving representing two Templars bringing down from this chamber the dead and half-naked body of their supposed victim.

At the same time it should be clearly understood that what chiefly calls for protest in this statement of Mr. Addison's, is not the charge of cruelty against the Templars, but the unscrupulous way in which a highly improbable conjecture is assumed as certain

---

[1] Perhaps we may except the cell of Edington Abbey Church, Wilts.

[2] They may be observed at St. Alban's, Westminster, Lichfield, Oxford, Worcester, and Canterbury. The same arrangement probably existed at Exeter and Lincoln.

[3] Another possible explanation is suggested by a passage in Viollet le Duc, *Dictionnaire de l'Architecture*, vol. viii. p. 4. "There may still be seen," he says, "in the church of Mas d'Azil (Ariège) a little cell formed in the thickness of the wall in which it was customary to confine a lunatic. This tiny cell only received light and air from the interior of the church. Everything was there certainly that could be needed to turn a sane person into a madman, but whether it was with any hope of curing these unfortunate beings that they were thus mewed up (*Chartres*) is more than I can tell."

fact. That a prisoner should be so severely treated during his confinement that he survived but eight weeks is an incident for which probably every country in Europe as late as the seventeenth century could have furnished scores of parallels. A grave suspicion, we may readily admit, rests upon the Order of the Templars, that the terrible accusations which led to their suppression were not in all cases without foundation. If so, there could be no ground for surprise if a body of rough soldiers who had lost their religious spirit should occasionally have set the law of the Church at defiance in the cruelty exercised upon offenders against their statutes. But even in the case of the Templars there is no reason for taking such charges for granted without reasonable proof, and neither here, nor in the human remains discovered at Temple Brewer, can we say that anything like a clear case has been made out against them.

It will be sufficient here again to appeal to the Protestant authority already referred to. "In other vaults," writes Archdeacon Churton, "under some of these ruins there have been found heaped together in confusion the remains of bodies of old men and children, and some with broken skulls, as if they had died by violence. This is described particularly as the case at an old ruin of a house of the Templars. Is it not most probable that these may be the bones of persons slain in the Wars of the Roses, or the later civil wars, and thrown into these vaults, as a place where they would be out of the way and none would interfere with them? The Templars were not accused by their worst enemies of making a kind of 'black hole' of any part of their premises. Nothing is more uncertain than a charge founded on the discovery of human bones in disused cemeteries and in unusual positions."[1]

The passing allusion that has lately been made to anchorets and recluses, suggests the interesting question how far a confused oral

---

[1] Op. cit. p. 314.

tradition about these voluntary prisoners may not be responsible for the popular belief in the existence of walled-up nuns. People had certainly not forgotten this institution of pre-Reformation days in the time of Shakspere. It is thus that the player-queen in *Hamlet* alludes to the practice:

> To desperation turn my trust and hope,
> An anchor's cheer in prison be my scope.

The life, no doubt, of these recluses was a severe one, and what Mr. Cutts calls "the popular idea that they inhabited a living grave,"[1] was occasionally, though rarely, to some extent justified.[2] Bilney, the Reformer, in his *Reliques of Rome* (1563), has a long indictment of the "monastical sect of recluses and such as be shutte up within walls, there unto death continuall to remayne," and we may remark that an interesting verbal parallel to Dr. Rule's bugbear may be found in the phrase used of an anchoret in a note to Peter Langtoft's Chronicle: *Richardus Fraunceys inter quatuor parietes pro Christo inclusus*—"Richard Francis enclosed between four walls for Christ's sake."[3]

We have no space here to discuss the question of recluses at any length, but it may be interesting to note the deep impression which the idea had evidently made upon the mediæval imagination. No book, perhaps, is more truly representative of the habit of mind of that epoch than the *Golden Legend,* and this is how we find the penance of "Thaysis" described in that collection of stories. I quote the translation of Caxton reproduced by Cutts. "She went to the place whiche th' abbot had assygned to her, and there was a monasterye of vyrgyns; and there he closed her in a

---

[1] *Scenes and Characters of the Middle Ages*, p. 121.

[2] *Ibid.* p. 146.

[3] Edit. Hearne, ii. 623.

celle and sealed the door with led. And the celle was lytyll and strayte, and but one lytell wyndowe open, by whych was mynistred to her poor livinge; for the Abbot commanded that they shold give to her a lytell brede and water." The great number of recluses in England during the middle ages has never perhaps been properly estimated. There seem to have been as many as a dozen living in the city of Norwich alone, all in separate anchor-holds. What is perhaps of importance in the present connection is that in some cases this enclosure was enjoined as a penance. The recluse remained a prisoner, but in this sense a voluntary prisoner that she was physically free to leave her cell if she chose. An instance is quoted by M. Viollet le Duc under the heading, *reclusoir.*

In a paper like the present it is almost inevitable that more hares should be started than it is possible to run down satisfactorily. Still there is one allusion which occurs in an extract given in an earlier page which I should be sorry to leave without some further comment, however brief. In the Rev. W. L. Holland's magic-lantern lecture on *Convents Romish and Anglican,* he tells his hearers, it may be remembered, that Dr. Grattan Guinness has "lately seen most perfect skeletons of walled-up nuns … in the old disused monasteries of Mexico." It would be interesting to have Dr. Grattan Guinness' own description before us, and with that object I have examined the list of the somewhat voluminous *opera omnia* of that reverend controversialist in the British Museum Catalogue, also the titles of the scarcely less voluminous works of Mrs. Grattan Guinness. However, none of these seem to promise anything about Mexico, and so I am forced to make at a venture a suggestion which may possibly account for this remarkable feature in Dr. Grattan Guinness' experiences.

It is a piece of information which seems to be tolerably familiar abroad, though it may possibly be new to some English readers, that the Capuchin Order in more southern climes have a peculiar custom as to the disposal of their dead. When a religious dies, the body is conveyed to a crypt or mortuary chapel under the church, and there, still clothed, in the habit, is fixed upright in a sort of niche, where it is carefully bricked up. A twelvemonth or so afterwards, generally before the feast of All Souls, the brick partition in front is removed, and the remains, of which by this time nothing is left but the skeleton, are exposed to view. The bones are draped in a new habit, and are then allowed to stand in the crypt side by side with many similar skeletons, where their religious brethren and the faithful come from time to time to pray for their souls. This somewhat ghastly spectacle[1] has been made the subject of a copy of verses by "C. C. G.," written, it appears, in 1830.[2] I reproduce the last three stanzas:

> Amidst the mould'ring relics of the dead,
>   In shapes fantastic which the brethren rear,
> Profaned by strangers' light unhallowed tread,
>   The monklike skeletons erect appear.
>
> The cowl is drawn each ghastly skull around,
>   Each fleshless form arrayed in sable vest;
> About their hollow loins the cord is bound,
>   Like living Fathers of the Order drest.
>
> And as the monk around this scene of gloom
>   The flickering lustre of his taper throws,
> He says, "Such, stranger, is my destined tomb;
>   Here, and with them, shall be my last repose."

Now it is not, I think, too much to assume that if Dr. Grattan

---

[1] I understand that both in Malta, where the "baked monks," as they were irreverently termed by the English passengers of the P. and O. steamers, were accounted among the sights of the island, and in the Capuchin convents of Italy, the practice is now forbidden.

[2] Printed in *The Catholic Keepsake*, p. 80. Burns and Oates.

Guinness had come upon a cemetery of this description, left probably *in statu quo* in some suppressed Capuchin convent in Mexico, the sight would certainly have presented in his eyes all the features of a horrible tragedy.

But if nuns were never walled-up alive, some reader may say, how is it that the story has come to be so widely believed? The limits of this pamphlet do not allow me to answer the question as fully as it deserves, although we have already glanced at some possible explanations. The etymological confusions of the word *immure,* the voluntary confinement of recluses, the manner of sepulture practised in some religious Orders, have all probably contributed something to the myth. But there remain many other causes to be taken into account. The upright interment of dead bodies is a practice not unknown even in England since the Reformation.[1] On the Continent burial alive was a common penalty for several classes of offences. More noteworthy still, a curious pagan superstition[2] survived for centuries in many countries of Europe that to secure the permanence of great structures—bridges, castles, or what not, it was necessary that the body of a child or a maiden should be built up into the foundations. In other cases doorways have been bricked up as the most convenient way of hiding the evidences of a tragedy.[3] When such things come to light bigotry has always an explanation ready, and the unknown terrors of the cloister are invoked to account for every skeleton found in an old building in an unusual position. But even could such allegations be proved in individual instances, as assuredly they have never been proved, the fact remains that the whole spirit of monasticism is in flagrant contradiction to them. Sir Walter Scott describes his three judges as

---

[1] See instances quoted by Peacock, l.c. pp. 50, 51.

[2] *Ibid.* p. 49, and *The Academy*, July 31, 1886, p. 73.

[3] The "secret chamber" of Glamis Castle is said to be a case in point.

> All servants of Saint Benedict
> The statutes of whose order strict
> On iron table lay.

"It is a pity," says the Protestant Archdeacon Churton, that this man of genius had not first read these statutes and seen how totally inconsistent is the spirit and the letter of them with such a doom as he describes."[1] This is really the main issue, and I can find no more suitable words than these with which to conclude this essay.

---

[1] Churton, l.c. p. 312.

*9 7 8 1 9 1 0 3 7 5 5 7 0 *